Introduction

He was considered mentally deficient by his teachers. Here is what one said: "Terribly slow. Often cannot repeat the question. Must concentrate." Said another, "Unless Dominic really shakes himself up and gets down to work, he is not going to achieve any success... he is painfully slow."

He agreed with the assessments. He writes in his book, "Although they might sound harsh, these reports paint a fairly accurate picture of my state of mind as a child." He hated school and dropped out as soon as he legally could.

Who was that slow child? He is Dominic O'Brien, eight-time World Memory Champion. Today he says of that time, "What a pity that I didn't discover and practice the art of memory when I was at school!"

What a pity indeed! Can you imagine what a man who once memorized the order of 54 packs of playing cards (2,808 cards, in case you were wondering) in one sitting could have done in school with such an incredible memory?

Does Dominic O'Brien have an incredibly high IQ? Is he a super genius? Here is what he says about his mental powers. "I wasn't born with any special gift. I started training when I was thirty."

How could this be? The fact is incredible memories are a skill just like any other skill: riding a bike, cooking, throwing a ball and so on. I have no doubt that Dominic O'Brien is a very smart guy, but no one is born with the ability to memorize the order of 2,808 playing cards in one sitting. A mental feat like that can only be accomplished with training and practice.

The good news is that you can quickly learn the same techniques that Dominic O'Brien used. It takes thousands of hours of practice to be a World Memory Champion, but **it only takes about an hour or so to dramatically improve your ability to memorize.** If you consistently use the techniques you will continue to get better and better. If you are a student you can have more free time for work or for your life outside of school. If you are a non-student you will soon have a tool to learn about subjects that have always interested you or to master material required for your job or hobby.

One Hour Memory Power is a very simple system to use. But do not be fooled by its simplicity. This is essentially the same system that Dominic

O'Brien and other World Memory Champions use. There is a slight difference, however. I have adapted the system to be more useful for learners rather than for use in memory competitions. In memory competitions the competitors learn the material and then recite it immediately. There is no need to remember the material for longer than an hour or so. Students, however may need to recall material in June that they learned in September! Also I have omitted any techniques that do not have a direct bearing on learning a subject such as memorizing a deck of cards, memorizing names and faces, and so on. These things are interesting and valuable in their own right but are not relevant for a student trying to master subject material.

I want to emphasize once again that memory techniques are a skill. Be sure to do the exercises and try to use the system every day for a month. You will be amazed at how quickly you can learn new material and at how long you will be able to retain what you have learned.

Before we start:

Underlined and bolded material emphasizes important points. Also at the end of every section is a take away section summarizing the main points in that section. You will get the most from this workbook if you make sure you pay special attention to the bolded points and the take away sections with the summary.

In the back of the workbook is an appendix. The appendix contains practice material. **I urge you to practice with the actual material you wish to memorize,** but if you want to ease into the techniques and try them out then the practice material is for you. There are a variety of short lists containing mostly abstract material such as foreign language words, science terms, and miscellaneous other items.

Materials needed now

But before we go any further, please take a moment and make sure you have everything needed to get the most from this workbook.

First, make sure you have one to two hours free without interruption and that you have a quiet place to work. Next you'll need a pen or pencil and a notebook or some paper. To be most effective, you should write the exercises yourself, on paper. Using a laptop or tablet to type exercises isn't as effective early on in the memory process, so I urge you to use the old-school tools of pen and paper first. This workbook has practice examples but by all means use school work, news stories, names or anything else you might want to learn.

One other thing. I know this is repetitious but I can't make the point strongly enough. To get the most out of this course **it is very, very important to do the example exercises. Memory techniques are a skill** like singing or dancing or playing baseball. Memory techniques are something you do, not something you just read about. The exercises are very easy, sometimes trivial, but don't let that fool you. Once you have actually practiced them you will find it very easy to apply them in real life. Moreover you can gain the skill in about one hour! So... do the example exercises.

How OHMP works: A quick overview of where we are headed

Our memory for images is much, much better than our memory for words or concepts. We are going to transform the information we want to remember into mental images and then, using our imagination, we will "place" those images in locations we have previously identified. A location can be anything. When we first start we will use locations around our neighborhood or spots in a room to place our images. With just a little bit of experience however we will be able to use anything that can be searched sequentially. This might be the position of players on a baseball field or football field or it could be various parts of an automobile or even our body.

When we want to recall the information we will simply review the locations. Our memory for images is so good that we will be able to mentally recall the image we placed at that location with very little trouble. The image will prompt us to recall the original information. If we wish to remember the information for a long time, such as a semester or two, we can review it at regular intervals to permanently fix it in our mind.

You will see in a few minutes that this memory technique is very easy to learn and it works much better then rote repetition. You will amaze yourself! That's it! Let's get started!

4 Steps to learning

There are 4 steps to leaning new material. The steps are:

Get it – **The information must enter our minds in order to remember it.**
This seems obvious but almost everyone has had the experience of day
dreaming while reading or watching TV. When we come out of our day
dream we have no idea what we have just read or seen. This section contains
two techniques to stay engaged and make sure we stay aware of what we are
trying to learn.

Create a mental file drawer – **Create a mental filing system so
information can be easily recalled.**   Fortunately this is very easy. We can
create unlimited filing space by using familiar spaces around us.

Picture it – **Transform the information into pictures and place the
pictures in your mental file drawer**. Our ability to remember pictures is
dramatically better than our ability to remember text, roughly twice as good
without practice. When combined with a memory system and practice, our
ability to remember is many, many times greater. This section details some
techniques to make memorable pictures from both concrete and abstract
material.

Review it – **The information must be reviewed periodically to be
retained**. For maximum effectiveness the time between review sessions
should grow progressively longer. You'll learn guidelines to calculate the
ideal duration between review periods.

Get It

Step one - Get it.

We need to pay attention to what we want to remember.

You are watching a basketball game. During the game a gorilla walks across the basketball court, through the action. Do you think you would notice? Don't be so sure.

In the book *Memory*, authors Richard F. Thompson and Stephen A. Madigan relate the story of an experiment involving people's focus and attention. Undergraduate students were asked to watch a video of an amateur basketball game where the players frequently passed the ball back and forth. The students were asked to keep separate tallies of the number of air passes or bounce passes. Because basketball is a fast moving game, and the ball is frequently passed back and forth, it required all of the students' attention to count the number of passes and to keep separate tallies. At some point in the basketball game, a person wearing a gorilla suit entered from the left, briefly faced the camera, pounded their chest, and exited to the right. When the game was finished the students were asked if they had noticed anything unusual. Only about half of the students noticed the person in the gorilla suit! The subjects were concentrating so hard on their task they failed to notice the other event happening during the game.

Most of us have had the experience of daydreaming while doing something else, reading or watching television or driving for example. When we stop daydreaming, we realize we were not aware of what went on around us while our minds were off in the clouds. We can't recall what happened during the TV show or what we have read. We were not aware, so therefore, we can't remember. Usually this is due to **fatigue or boredom. Both cause our minds to wander.**

On the other hand, if the material is interesting to us we have no trouble staying engaged, provided we have had adequate sleep and rest. If we are interested in cars and we are reading a car magazine we normally have no problem staying engaged in the material. If we are interested in fashion and we are reading a fashion magazine we will pay attention to what we are reading. The reverse is also true. If we are interested in fashion and we are required to read about cars for a class we will have trouble keeping our minds from wandering.

We cannot remember anything until it enters our consciousness. **To say it another way, we have to be consciously aware of what we want to remember.** If the material we need to learn is boring or if we are too tired, then we have to take special care to make sure we are aware of what we are learning.

Two strategies to help awareness

There are two strategies you can use to make yourself aware of what you want to remember. The first is simply to **describe out loud what is happening**. For example, if you're a person who frequently misplaces their keys or purse, a good strategy to help you remember where you left them, is to say aloud as you put them down "I am putting my purse on the desk" or "I am leaving my cell phone in my pants pocket". This will make you aware of what you are doing and thus much more likely to remember it later. This simple technique can also work for things you wish to remember in the future. For example, you might consciously say out loud, "I need to call the bank when I get to the office". **Being mindful of what you are doing, or want to do, greatly helps recall.**

The second strategy is to **ask questions or make observations about what is going on**. This is especially important if what you are trying to learn is boring. Everyone has a difficult time remembering boring material. If you hate history you will have a hard time keeping yourself from daydreaming while you are reading a history textbook. For any textbook, a good strategy is to flip through the pages of the reading assignment first, skimming the material and making observations or asking questions formulated on the headings or illustrations. Keep these observations and questions in mind as you go back and read the material. For a movie or video or novel, try to ask questions about the motivations of the characters or try to predict what will happen next. "Does she hate him?" "Why is he going into the storm? Is this foreshadowing?" **The important thing is to get consciously involved in the subject by asking questions.**

Take Away

We need to be consciously aware of what we want to remember

Fatigue and boredom cause our minds to wander.

Two ways to prevent daydreaming or spacing out

1. Describe out loud what is happening
2. Ask questions or make observations about what you are reading or seeing

Create a Mental
File Drawer

Step two - Create a mental file drawer

We need to organize the information we want to remember so we can systematically search for it later.

Imagine we hear about a new library in our town. When we go there we discover the books are placed at random on the library shelves. In order to find a specific book we have to search through all of the shelves until we stumble across what we are looking for.

Our memories are somewhat like that library. Unless we have made a specific effort to categorize our memories we have to think about random associations in order to recall what we are trying to remember. For example, if we are trying to remember a person's name we might try to recall what they were wearing, where we were introduced to them, the time of day we met them, or the weather and so on, hoping that these random associations will connect us to the person's name.

In a regular library however, the books are all organized according to the Dewey decimal system. If we know what book we are looking for we can look up its number in the book catalog and then go directly to the shelf where it is located and find the book.

It is much easier to find items in our memory if they are nicely organized rather than haphazardly placed. Most of us organize our memories according to time. First this happened, next, the other thing happened. First, there was a car accident, then the police came. While this technique is fine for events that happen in real time it doesn't work very well for material we wish to memorize.

As mentioned before, we are going to transform the material we wish to memorize into images. We will then organize our images so we can easily review them. Fortunately for us there is a very simple way to organize our images - by location. We can use the natural order of our neighborhood, or the natural order of items in a room, as places to store the images we create. For example, as I look clockwise around my family room I have a fireplace, a basket above the fireplace, a dog bed in the corner, and so on. Here are the first 10 items in my family room which I always review in sequence.

Family Room

1. Just outside door
2. Just inside door
3. Fireplace
4. Basket above fireplace
5. Dog bed
6. Ethiopia poster
7. Left window
8. Bookcase
9. TV
10. Right window

I use this list to store images. Here's how. If I want to remember to buy a loaf of bread, a carton of milk and a newspaper I can imagine a loaf of bread just outside the door to the family room (#1 on the mental map of my family room), a carton of milk just inside the door (#2 on the mental map) and a newspaper in the fireplace (#3 on the mental map). We will cover this in detail in the next section but for now we will just think about the lists.

We will refer to these lists we use to organize our images as file drawers. Each item in the list will be referred to as a file folder. In the real world you might place something you wish to remember into a file folder and then place the folder into a file drawer. In the mental world we have a list of locations which corresponds to a file drawer. We will transform what we want to remember into a mental image and then associate that image with a location. **The location represents the file folder and the list of locations represents the file drawer.** In the example above, items in my family room, the list itself is the file drawer and individual items like the fireplace or the dog bed are referred to as the file folders. **Whenever you read 'file drawer' know that we are referring to a list of locations that you can search sequentially in your memory. Whenever you read 'file folder' know**

that we are referring to individual items in the list. Many times this is a series of locations like the locations in my family room but **anything you know well, which you can mentally review in a logical order and standard sequence , will work just fine.**

The first thing to note is I **have written down in a notebook the items** in my family room **that I want to use for a filing system**. If you are a student, you will, over time, have several, perhaps many, mental file drawers or lists of locations. File drawers can be items in your dorm room, places in a lecture hall, or locations in a cafeteria. **It is important to go over the list in the same order every time**. By reviewing in the same order every time you will be sure nothing is overlooked and you will also know if you have forgotten an image stored at a location. Also, if you have written down your locations, you can easily page through your notebook, pick a mental file drawer to use for the memory task at hand, and review that list to make sure that you are absolutely certain of the correct order. Of course, the list should be very familiar to you. The reason to review is to make sure exactly what items you have included or not included in any particular list. "Did I include the dog bed in my family room file drawer?"

The second thing to note is I have underlined the words 'outside' and 'inside' in the first two locations. This is to remind me of the fact that the two locations are very similar and could easily be confused in my memory unless I take special precautions to keep them separate. Use this technique whenever you have locations that are not totally distinct from one another as, for example, the four corners of a table or a row of chairs. In general you should try to make your locations as distinct as possible so there is no possibility of confusing them in your mind when you review.

The last thing to note is that I have gone around my family room in a clockwise (or left to right) manner and, where items are in the same vertical plane, I have gone bottom to top. In other words standing just inside the door the fireplace is the next item on my list (to my left or clockwise) and the basket above the fireplace (bottom to top) is the second next item on my list. Always reviewing your list in the same order helps make sure no item is overlooked.

Exercise one – create a list of locations to store our images
Now it's your turn. Look around the room you are in and choose at least 12

distinct places in the room to file images. Write down the locations and number them on a piece of paper or in your notebook. If you see more than twelve places you could use, that is just fine, but try to get at least 12 because we will use 12 locations in our next exercise.

Here are the 20 places in my family room that I use, always in this sequence. I could easily have added 20 more locations if I had needed them by including lamps, heat registers, shelves on a bookcase and so on.

Just <u>outside</u> door
Just <u>inside</u> door
Fireplace
Basket over fireplace
Dog bed
Ethiopia poster
Left window
Bookcase
TV
Right window
Art print "Red face"
Wall phone
Counter
Recliner
Recliner footstool
Beanbag chair
Bottom snowshoe
Top snowshoe
Brown chair
Brown chair footstool

Of course these locations are unique to me just as your locations are unique to you. Usually this doesn't make any difference but there is one exception. Suppose you are studying the same material with someone else. Perhaps you are trying to help a child learn the states. Perhaps you are in the same class with a group of students who have also read *One Hour Memory Power*. In these cases you will need to have a community file drawer so you can review the same locations with the same images.

Take Away

Write down your lists so you can review as needed

Always go through the file drawer in same order
    In a room review left to right and bottom to top

Make sure you distinguish between similar locations such as corners of a table, inside or outside a door

Picture it

Step three - Picture it

Use your terrific memory for pictures

As we mentioned before, your memory for images is extremely good. This effect has been studied and confirmed so many times psychologists have given the effect its own name, The Pictorial Superiority Effect or PSE for short. Right off the bat, without practice, your image memory is roughly twice as good as your memory for verbal material. The good news is, the more you practice using images to remember material the better you will become.

Some things are naturally easy to visualize. Look around the room where you are sitting and everything you see, you could visualize easily. You could close your eyes and have a mental picture of the objects in the room. You might see a desk, a chair, a picture and so on. All of these things are easily visualized because they are real objects that we see every day. The good thing about using mental images that we visualize is we can change them in our imagination to make them more memorable. For example, you have a pen or pencil in your workspace now. An ordinary pen or pencil is not very memorable. The physical pen cannot change but in our mind's eye we can make the pencil as big as a skyscraper or as small as a needle. Now that would be memorable! The pen is probably made of plastic but in our imagination we can have the pen made out of stainless steel or gold or wood or a squishy piece of rubber or ...you get the idea. In our imaginations, in our mind's eye, we can "see" or visualize images that would be impossible in real life. These "impossible" images are much easier to remember.

Here is a quick exercise. Take a moment, close your eyes and imagine your pen or pencil as big as a skyscraper. See it in your mind's eye. This ability to imagine impossible things and scenes is vital to developing our super memory. **The brain remembers imaginary images almost as well as real images.** If, in reality, we saw a pen as large as a skyscraper we would never forget it. If we imagine a pen as large as a skyscraper we will remember it for a long time. We will remember the image much longer than we will remember the phrase "a pen as big as a skyscraper".

As you form images, do not make judgments about how good or correct an image might be. It might be natural to think a pen could never be as large as a skyscraper, but in our imaginations, it can be. Moreover the image is memorable, which is what we want.

Picturing abstract images

All students, whether formally enrolled in school or not, will encounter many concepts that at first glance seem to be difficult to visualize. Subjects such as economics, religion, philosophy, psychology, sociology and many others are filled with abstract concepts. These might include concepts such as truth, freedom, justice, the economy, good, evil, politics and so on.

You might think it would be difficult or impossible to picture abstract concepts, but in reality, with very little practice, you will be able to do it automatically, almost without thinking. Let's learn the first five presidents of the United States as an example.

Almost all names are abstract. What does a Washington look like? The name itself is almost impossible to visualize. The good news is we can think of a concrete image that represents Washington and that concrete image will be easy to remember. After we think of an image to represent Washington we can then associate that image with the first location in our list we just made.

The first five presidents of the United States were:

Washington
Adams
Jefferson
Madison
Monroe

There are two different strategies we can use to picture these presidents. **The first technique is to imagine something that sounds like the word we wish to remember.** We simply imagine a concrete item that sounds somewhat like the abstract word or concept we wish to remember. For example, for George Washington we might picture a huge **washing** machine able to hold a **ton** of clothes at one time.

The second strategy is to think of an image that symbolizes the word we wish to remember. We might picture a fireworks display to represent the 4th of July. We might picture a judge in heavy black robes sitting in a courtroom pounding a gavel to represent the abstract concept of law. For George Washington we might imagine a general dressed in a Revolutionary war uniform inspecting his troops. Both techniques work equally well and they can be freely mixed and matched for any given idea or word.

A few other things to keep in mind as you form images. We don't remember boring things very well because ...well, they are boring. **As you create mental images it is important to try to make them as memorable as possible**. This makes the image interesting to you so you are more likely to recall it.

Try to come up with an image for each of the presidents then turn the page and see my suggestions.

Washington – A great big washing machine able to hold a ton of clothes

Adams – an atom bomb exploding or simply an atom

Jefferson – A intercity bus (in the USA Jefferson is the second largest bus line) or Jeff's son

Madison – a Mad Son – a young man having a temper tantrum

Monroe – a man rowing

Don't worry if your images don't match mine or even are wildly different than mine. **A stumbling block** for many people first learning a mnemonic system **is to overthink the task and spend a lot of time unnecessarily trying to make "good" images. Realize that whatever image the word Washington triggered in your mind will probably be the same image that will come to mind the next time you come across the word Washington.**

Use the first image that occurs to you and don't try to make it perfect, at least at first. Try to make your images vivid and distinct rather than "good". After you have reviewed your list a few times, if you find that some images are especially difficult to recall, then take a few minutes and try to come up with a better image. I think you will find you do not have to do this very often.

Five ways to enhance images to make them more memorable.

You can use **motion**. For example, in our next exercise we will memorize the mascots of the Pacific Athletic Conference (PAC 12). We will use the University of Arizona to illustrate. Their mascot is a wild cat. You could picture the wildcat jumping up and down, running, waving its arms or some other motion.

Emotion is another effective way of making memorable images. You might think the wildcat is mean, cuddly, hateful, or any one of other emotions. The important point is that if you have a feeling about an image, magnify the emotion and attach it to the image.

Size is another way to add to the memorability of an image. You could imagine the wildcat very large, perhaps two or three stories tall "the wildcat that ate the stadium." Or you could imagine the wildcat very small, so small that the wildcat could fit in the palm of your hand.
Related to size is the **exaggeration of certain features** in the image. You might imagine the wildcat with great big huge paws, or ears or huge sharp teeth.

Lastly, **bizarre** images are remembered more easily than boring images. For example instead of imagining the wildcat as a mascot at a football or basketball game, you could imagine a football player being the mascot while five Wildcats were playing basketball. This is highly unlikely but it would be memorable!
Whenever possible add motion, emotion, size, exaggerated features or some bizarre characteristic or situation to make your images memorable.

Take Away

Imagined images are remembered almost as well as real images

With abstract words create an image by using:
1. A sound alike word - tooth for truth
2. An image that symbolizes the concept - fireworks for 4th of July

Add motion, emotion, size, exaggerated features or some bizarre characteristic or situation to make your images memorable. Try to

make images vivid and distinct.

The first image that comes to mind is frequently the best. Revise it later if need be.

Place Pictures
Into
File Folders

Step four - Place images into mental file folders

We have created a list of locations and we have created some mental images to represent the first five presidents of the United States. Now we can combine the images with the locations. For example, as I create images such as the huge washing machine to represent President Washington, I can imagine that washing machine sitting right outside my family room door, the first location on my list. Later, when I wish to recall the image, I simply have to think of the space just outside my family room and the image of the washing machine will automatically come to mind and remind me of George Washington.

Next, moving sequentially down the list of file folders which I made using objects in my family room, I would think of the space just inside the family room door. In this space I might imagine a miniature mushroom cloud because a super tiny atomic bomb just exploded. This would remind me of John Adams. For the third item in my family room I could imagine a tiny model of a city to city bus – a Jefferson bus – in the fireplace burning up. When I think of the fireplace I would see in my mind's eye the tiny Jefferson bus which would remind me of Thomas Jefferson. Monroe would be represented by a man rowing a boat which I imagine in the basket hanging on the wall. Next I would think of the dog bed and, again in my mind's eye, I would see my uncle (my family name is Madison and my uncle was a terrific singer) standing on the dog bed singing. Whenever I envision the dog bed I will automatically think of my uncle which will remind of James Madison.

Exercise Two, Part One - PAC-12 Mascots

This is the first part of a two part exercise.
Look at the mental file drawer you just wrote down. For each location, write down each one of the mascots.
Here are the mascots:

Wildcats
Sun Devils
Golden Bears
Ducks
Beavers
Trojans

Cardinals
Bruins
Huskies
Cougars
Buffaloes
Utes (The Ute are a Native American tribe)

My list looks like this:

1. Just <u>outside</u> door   Wildcat
2. Just <u>inside</u> door   Sun Devil
3. Fireplace   Golden Bear

Now fill out your list with the mascots.
This is very important. Do not skip this step. Review the list using your imagination to picture each location with the mascot in that location. For example, I could picture a Wildcat just outside the door of my family room and a Sun Devil just inside the door. Go through the entire list this way picturing a mascot at each location.

When you have finished, close your eyes or look away from your list and review each location and each mascot at that location. **Forgetting begins immediately when you stop studying. An immediate review or two, from memory, consolidates what you have learned and will tremendously help your later recall.** If it helps your concentration say the list out loud or, if you are in a library or other quiet place, you can just mouth the words. When you can do this twice, without error, move on to the next exercise.

Exercise Two, Part Two – PAC-12 mascots

This is the second part of the exercise we just completed. We are going to add the mascot's school to the list we just memorized. We will use two different techniques as we do this.
Here are the PAC-12 mascots and their schools:

Wildcats, Arizona
Sun Devils, Arizona State
Golden Bears, California
Ducks, Oregon
Beavers, Oregon State

Trojans, Southern California
Cardinals, Stanford
Bruins, UCLA
Huskies, Washington
Cougars, Washington State
Buffaloes, Colorado
Utes, Utah

The first technique is to link one image to another by imaging the two images interacting. In this case the first image will be the mascot and the second image will be the school. Of course, the Universities cannot be easily pictured like the mascots because they are abstract. We will need to make up and use a substitute word for each university. We will then put the combined image in the appropriate location in our list.

A fun and easy way to imagine the images interacting is to **make up a story about each combined image.** For example, you might imagine the Arizona Wildcat insulted a fan of the opposing team, was chased around the stadium before he escaped, and now has to stand in front of a big huge fan in the "air zone" (Arizona) to cool down so he doesn't suffer heat stoke! Psychologists call this technique progressive elaboration. **Adding some details to an image or creating a little story around the image will help you remember the image longer.**

The next technique is to write out the locations, images and mascots and arrange them into a grid.
Write out your Memory Grid™ like this: Here is an example of the first three mascots.

Location

1. Just <u>outside</u> door

2. Just <u>inside</u> door

3. Fireplace

4.

I mage
Wildcat standing in front of a huge fan (Airy Zone)

Sun Devil sticking a steak into the blades of another big fan (Airy Zone Steak)

Bright yellow bear with surfboard curled up in fireplace taking a Nap

Mascot & University
Wildcat – Arizona

Sun Devil – Arizona State

Golden bear – California

Of course you can type out the Memory Grid™ as well as write it by hand. How you do it doesn't matter, just so you do it yourself, in some way.

Location	Image	Mascot and University
1. Just <u>outside</u> door	Wildcat standing in front of huge fan (Airy Zone)	Wildcat - Arizona
2. Just <u>inside</u> door	Sun Devil sticking a stake into the blades of another big fan (Airy Zone Steak or stake if that makes a better image for you)	Sun Devil - Arizona State
3. Fireplace	Bright yellow bear with surfboard (California) curled up in the fireplace taking a nap.	Golden Bear - California (Berkley)
4. Basket		
5. Dog bed		
Etc.		

Now take a few minutes and complete the grid your own way.

Perhaps a natural question to ask is why put a Memory Grid™ on paper if we are going to memorize the material. We will talk about this at length in the review section but the short answer is that we will be reviewing this material at ever-increasing time periods. Even though this memory technique is very, very good it is not perfect. It is possible, even probable, that one or two items will be forgotten. If you are a student you may have to recall, on your final exam in June, material which you were taught in September! That is a long time. **Having a written out Memory Grid™ allows for a quick and easy review of all elements; the mental file drawer, the material we wish to remember, and the images we use to encode that material.**

Take away

Place an image of what you want to remember at each location on your list.

Link images together by imagining them interacting. One way to do that is to make up a quick story.

Be sure to make a MemoryGrid™ - write out your locations, images and the material you are memorizing. Going over the MemoryGrid™ is an excellent way to review.

Review once or twice immediately after making your MemoryGrid™

More
on
Mental File
Folders

When and how to use linked images

In our last exercise we only had two images, mascot and school, but in theory we could have many images. If we had more images we would imagine the first image interacting with the second image. We then imagine the second image interacting with the third image, the third with the fourth and so on until all the images are linked together. Using this technique you can easily get into the 'teens or even low twenties for the number of images linked.

This is extremely useful if you only have a list with 10 locations but you have 30 items you wish to remember. In that case you could link 3 items at the first location, three more at the second location, three more at the third location and so on. Linking is an effective way to multiply the size of your list.

There is a danger to linking however. **If you forget one link in the series you may be unable to continue because each image is tied to the next.** However, with a mental file drawer, if you forget an image stored at a particular location you can just go on to the next location. You are not blocked from remembering the rest of the material. For students, it is best not to link more than five items per location in the list unless you are supremely confident in how well you know the memory links. Remember you will need to recall your material during exams. For most people this is a high stress environment and, on top of it, you may be tired from staying up late studying. **Use linked images with caution.**

There is one exception where linked images make sense, and that would be where the same information is required for each item. Suppose we need to learn about the American presidents. The information we are required to learn is the same for every president; name, party, vice-president, and wife's name. You could create a Memory Grid™ for each president and then link the remaining items to each other with a complex image.

For example, your Memory Grid™ might look like this.

Location   Name/Party/Vice-President / Wife's Name Images
1. Just <u>outside</u> door   Washington / Federalist / John Adams / Martha
    washing machine, federal courthouse, atom bomb, Martha Stewart cookie

A huge washing machine sits on the steps of a federal courthouse. An atom bomb is stuck inside the washing machine and a Martha Stewart cookie is on top of the atom bomb.

2. Just <u>inside</u> door   John Adams / Federalist / Thomas Jefferson / Abigail
   atom bomb, federal courthouse, Jefferson bus, A big gale.
An atom bomb is driving a Jefferson bus up the steps of a federal courthouse. In the distance, dark clouds are forming because a big gale (Abigail) is coming.

There are a few things to notice in this example.   Normally when you create a series of linked images and you forget one of the links, you are unable to continue past the forgotten link. In this case however, **because the linked images for each president are always in the same order, Name, Party, Vice-President and wife's name, you can move to the next image if you forget one item in the series.** If you forget Washington's party you know that the next item in the series is vice-president so you can move on and try to recall that image.

The second thing to notice is the **elements of your image** i.e. the washing machine, the federal courthouse, the atom bomb and the Martha Stewart cookie **do not have to be in any particular order**. There is nothing wrong with them being in order, however it is very unlikely you will confuse the atom bomb representing Vice-President John Adams with the image representing Washington's wife Abigail.
Lastly make note of the fact that the **complex images are stored in the Memory Grid™ just as a single image would be**. Using my family room as an example, the image of a washing machine, atom bomb, federal courthouse and Martha Stewart cookie would be stored just outside the family room door.

Some other types of information that would lend themselves to this type of linking would be chemistry and the periodic table of the elements where a specific set of facts must be learned about each atom. Biology is another candidate for this type of linking where a plant or animal is fitted into ever broader classifications such as order, family, genus, species and so on.

Creating mental file drawers

What can be used to create mental file drawers? In a word, almost anything!

The only requirement is you are able to search it sequentially. Here are some examples of mental file drawers that most people are familiar with.

Rooms, as we have seen, are quick and ready options to use for file drawers. Any kind of room will do if it has enough distinguishing features. There are enough different kinds of rooms that there is no problem finding a place to use. Your favorite bar, coffee shop, convenience store, restaurant, and a friend's house are just a few of the many possibilities.

Another easy way to create a mental file drawer is to just walk around your neighborhood. Simply pick out distinct locations that you can easily traverse in your mind. You might pick a playground where there are many pieces of equipment. The many parts of each piece of equipment could also serve as the basis for a file drawer. Workout equipment in a gym could also be used.

Sports can also provide good lists. Remember we only need a sequence that we know well and that we can review in our minds. Baseball is a good example. At any given time there are 10 players on the field; the batter, catcher and pitcher, four infielders and three outfielders. These players stand in more or less the same positions every time so we can use their positions as file folders in the mental file drawer.

To use the first item from our last exercise I could image the catcher being a wildcat. Next to the wildcat is a fan blowing on him. It doesn't even need to be that complicated. I could simply place the image of the wildcat and fan on top of the catcher's head. I could place the next image on the batter's head and so on.

With a little knowledge of baseball and a little elaboration you can turn the 10 locations into 20 by adding the four umpires, the two base coaches, the two foul poles and the two dugouts. If you use a baseball team as a file drawer, remember to always review it in the same order every time.
Another sports example might be either American or world football. In each case there are twenty–two players on the field and, if you are somewhat knowledgeable about the game, you could elaborate on that number just as we did with baseball.

Here are some more ideas.
Cricket – There are 15 on the field – eleven fielders plus two batsmen and

two umpires for a total of 15
The human body – Many, many possible spots to make a list.
Automobile or motor bike - Like the human body, with many possible spots.
A band or orchestra - Each member could be a location and their instruments could also serve as locations.

How many mental file drawers can I have or do I need?

The easy answer is you can have an unlimited number of lists and you should create as many as you need. As a guideline, on the top end, Dominic O'Brien, an eight time world memory champion, has 100 lists, each 52 locations long or a total of 5200 locations. He uses 50 of them for memory competitions and the other 50 are reserved for facts he wishes to remember such as sports facts, music hits, political items and so on.

In my own case, a normal adult, non-student, who follows sports, technology and politics, I have about 150 locations in 6 different file drawers and, for me, that is sufficient. When I want to remember new material I simply reuse one of my lists.

If you are a secondary or college student you will probably want to be somewhere in between these two goalposts. One possible solution is to create a file drawer in each building you have a class. For example, if you have a chemistry class, create a list in the classroom or building where you have the class. If you have an art class, create a list in the classroom or studio where you have the art class.

Take Away

Use linked images with caution

If you forget one item in a series of linked images you may be unable to continue

If the same information is required over and over linked images may be useful
e.g In biology: Order, Family, Genus, species, etc.

Anything that can be mentally reviewed, in sequence, can be used as a mental file drawer.

Review it

Here is a trick question. Suppose you learn a word list just well enough so that you can repeat it without errors. The question is this, how long will it take you to forget half of the words? It is a trick question because, unless you already know the answer, you wouldn't guess it. In about 20 minutes or so you will have forgotten almost half of the words! At the end of the first day you will have forgotten almost two-thirds of the list! **Initial forgetting is dramatic and begins immediately when you stop** going over the material. The good news is that after the first day or so forgetting begins to slow down. After a month your memory for the word list will be almost the same as it was after two days. The forgetting curve looks like this. The bottom left line is the forgetting curve for someone who has just learned the list well enough to repeat it. The lines above represent forgetting after reviewing the material.

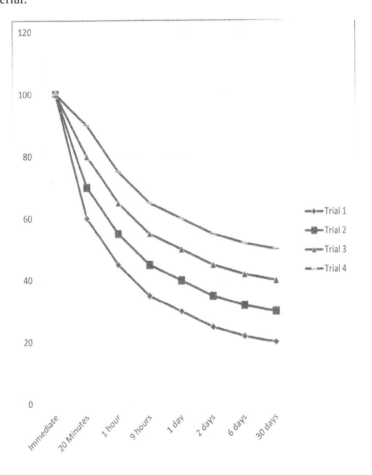

Placing images at specific locations will help a lot but won't completely solve the problem. In order to counteract this rapid forgetting we need to start our review process immediately when we stop studying. These initial reviews are critical to minimizing our relearning time later. **Memories are very fragile during the first few hours, so it is important to "cement" the images in your mind right away.**
As soon as you have finished filling out your Memory Grid™ with the images you have chosen, look away from the Memory Grid and mentally go through the list and recall each image. If you have trouble remembering the image at any location, use your Memory Grid™ as a refresher. Do this a few times or until you are absolutely confident that you can recall the material without an error.
Review mentally again after one or two hours. The images should still be clear in your mind. If you have trouble recalling any image, refresh your memory by reviewing with the Memory Grid™. Try to keep the images fresh in your mind for the first couple of days. A review while you are waiting to fall asleep is an excellent time for review as sleep seems to consolidate memories.

On day two, review sometime in the morning, soon after you get up, if possible, and then once again the evening. At this point, you should have reviewed your Memory Grid™ at least five times, three or more times on the first day and two or more times on the second day. Let me add a note here. Not only is everyone's memory different but also the material you are studying may be interesting or boring. Boring material is harder to remember so you may need to review more or less than these guidelines Perhaps you will need to review ten times the first day and five times the second day. On the other hand, perhaps the subject is intensely interesting to you in which case you only need to review once the first day and once the second day. **The important thing to remember is to keep the images fresh in your mind during the first few days. Don't let the images or meanings fade.**

One big advantage of the MemoryGrid™ is that you can review whenever you have a spare moment. Walking to class, waiting for an appointment, stuck in traffic and similar "dead" times are ideal for mental review.

On day three be sure to review again.

After these first few days you can start to space out the time between reviews.

Here is a rough timetable for reviewing average material. After the review on day three, use the following table to schedule your reviews.
Skip two days and review again on day five.
Skip three days
Skip five days
Skip ten days
Review again after a couple of weeks
After a month
After six weeks
After three months
After six months
Yearly thereafter.

Like the first few reviews, the time you wait between reviews varies from person to person and from subject to subject. These guidelines are not carved in stone so feel free to adjust them as needed. As always, if you have forgotten the image for a specific location, be sure to pull out your Memory Grid™ and review it. Most portals, such as Yahoo or Google, have calendars which you can configure to send yourself reminders of review dates. I have used both Yahoo and Google calendars but there are many others on the web which would work equally well.

Take Away

New memories are VERY fragile when first learned. Review immediately after completing the Memory Grid™ until you can recall the list mentally without forgetting anything.

Keep the images fresh in your mind the first few days then review periodically thereafter.

Make use of downtime and short, spare moments to mentally review your MemoryGrids.

Reviewing while waiting to fall asleep may be useful as some research indicates sleep may consolidate memories.

Numbers

Most mnemonic systems for remembering numbers are complex and, although they work, are not worth taking the time to learn. These methods work well but it takes a fair amount of up front time to master them. Otherwise, here is a very simple, but effective, system for coding numbers.

For numbers 1 to 10 a simple rhyming system works well. Each number can be visualized by imagining a word that rhymes with the number. For example, you could visualize the number one by picturing a gun or a bun. The number two could be represented by the image of a shoe. Here is the complete list:

Number rhyme system

0. Hero,   Nero
1. gun,   bun
2. shoe,   glue
3. tree,   flea
4. door,   store
5. Hive,   chive
6. sticks,   bricks
7. heaven,   Kevin
8. gate,   bait
9. vine,   wine
10. hen,   Big Ben (a famous clock and clock tower in London)

Every number is represented by two concrete images that rhyme, more or less, with the number. For example, the number one is represented by **either** gun **or** bun. The images are interchangeable. In similar fashion, the number two is represented by **either** shoe **or** glue. **Spend a few minutes picturing the number rhymes in order so you will always know what number rhyme is in the first column and which number rhyme is in the second column.**

To remember a number, combine the first number rhyme image with the second number rhyme image and then store that image in a mental file folder. **The word in the first column always represents the first number and the word in the second column always represents the second number.** For example, the number 16 would be gun-bricks, the number 32 would be tree-glue and the number 75 would be heaven-chive.

Let's take a couple of examples to illustrate how this works.

The Civil War in the U.S. started in 1861 and didn't end until 1865. Most U.S. students will know that the Civil War occurred sometime in the 1800s, so they only have to remember the numbers 61 and 65.

For the number 61 we can imagine sticks in between the halves of a hamburger bun. If we wanted to elaborate on this image we could imagine someone in a Civil War uniform biting down on this hamburger made of sticks and crying out in surprise when their teeth hit a stick. Because the word sticks is in the first column we know that 6 is the first number and since bun is in the second column we know that 1 is the second number.

For the number 65 we could imagine someone in a Civil War uniform poking sticks into a clump of chives growing in a herb garden. The person has developed a hatred for chives and is declaring war on them by poking the chives with sticks. Like the example above, we know that 6 is the first number and 5 is the second number because sticks is the word in the first column and chives is the word in the second column.

Let's take one more example. The Magna Carta was first signed in 1215. We would form an image of gun-glue and store it in our first file folder and then we would form a second image of gun-chive and then store it in our second location.. We won't confuse the order of the numbers because we know gun represents the first number of the pair and glue the second number of the pair. When recalling the second pair of numbers we know gun is the first number and chives represents the second number.

Take Away

A simple number rhyme system works for most numbers.

For lists less than 10 use the number-rhymes in the first column.

For double digit lists the rhyme in the first column represents the first number in the pair and the second number-rhyme represents the second number in the pair.

For three digit and longer numbers, break the number apart into pairs and store each pair in a location.

Wrap Up

In wrapping up, I'd like to emphasize a few key points that most memory books only touch on.

Because memory is a skill, the more you use these techniques the better you will become. Truly amazing feats have been accomplished using these or similar techniques. A gentleman in India has memorized over 30,000 digits of Pi. Another gentleman in Malaysia has memorized an entire Chinese/English dictionary of 1,774 pages and 57,000 words. Many people are able to go through a deck of cards once memorizing the entire order. You probably don't want to memorize a Chinese/English dictionary or even the order of a deck of cards, but the point is you can become very, very good at memorizing. The key is simply to practice. So... practice, practice, practice. Of course, if you are a student using these techniques every day is excellent practice.

As you review, be sure to look away from your material as you recall it. It is easy and tempting to look at your Memory Grid™ as you review but unaided recall is much, much more effective in cementing the material in your mind.

Most ads for memory books and courses sound as if you will be perfect every time you attempt to learn something. However, the reality is, the more you are trying to memorize, the greater the chance that you will forget one or two items. If, for example, you have 100 images you have learned you will probably find there are five or ten images that are difficult for you, especially the first time you try to recall them. Usually this is because the images were not vivid enough. Concentrate on making the image vivid by using the five techniques we mentioned earlier: motion, emotion, size, exaggerated features, and making the image bizarre. You can also add detail to the image such as color, sound, smell and so on.

Inevitably you're going to come across items that will be extremely difficult for you to remember. The images and what they represent just don't seem to stick in your mind. Depending on the subject you're studying, and how important it is to remember that particular piece of information, you can either just accept the fact that you won't be able to remember that particular piece of information or spend a lot more time creating a new image and/or spend more time reviewing your existing image. Anything can be memorized but some things might take an inordinate amount of time and energy. If the subject is not that important, sometimes it is just better to give up and move on.

Lastly, I hope you will have fun using these techniques and that they make a difference in your life as a student. I know they made a huge difference in my life both as a student and in my professional life.
Good Luck and, one last time, practice!

Appendix
Practice Material

This appendix contains 30 practice exercises divided into two groups. The first 15 relate to the real world in some way. They range from fairly easy, for example, the seven ways to classify dogs, to fairly difficult, the seven states that make up the United Arab Emirates. The last 15 exercises are lists of 10 randomly chosen words.

I encourage you to practice your memory skill every day. Of course, the best practice is to use material you actually wish to learn. Sometimes however that is not always possible. You may be a student during the summer or between semesters without access to your subject material. You may be a professional planning to attend a conference where you will need to learn large amounts of information. In cases like this you can use the practice material to hone your skills in preparation for the time you will need to use them.

Good luck!

One

The Seven Deadly Sins

Pride
Sloth
Wrath
Envy
Gluttony
Lust
Avarice

Two

12 signs of the zodiac

Aries
Taurus
Gemini
Cancer
Leo
Virgo
Libra
Scorpio
Sagittarius
Capricorn
Aquarius
Pisces

Three

10 provinces and 2 territories of Canada

Provinces
Alberta
British Columbia
Manitoba
New Brunswick
Newfoundland and Labrador
Nova Scotia
Ontario
Prince Edward Island
Québec
Saskatchewan

Territories
Northwest Territories
Yukon

Four

Nine planets

Mercury
Venus
Earth
Mars
Jupiter
Saturn
Uranus
Neptune
Pluto (may or may not be a planet)

Five

Santa's original eight reindeer (Before Rudolph)

Dasher
Dancer
Prancer
Vixen
Comet
Cupid
Donner
Blitzen

Six

Seven Habits of Highly Effective People by Stephen Covey

Be proactive (use initiative)
Begin with the end in mind (express and follow your vision)
Put first things first (prioritize)
Think win /win (find solutions that are mutually beneficial)
Seek first to understand, then be understood (the method for working towards a win/win solution)
Synergize (find creative new solutions)
Sharpen the saw (practice what you've learned)

Seven

United Arab Emirates

Abu Dhabi
Ajman
Dubai
Fujairah
Ras al-Khaimah
Sharjah
Umm al-Qaiwain

Eight

Snow White and the Seven Dwarfs

Bashful
Doc
Dopey
Grumpy
Happy
Sleepy
Sneezy

Nine

Seven classifications of dogs

herding dogs
hounds
non-sporting dogs
sporting dogs
terriers
toys
working dogs

Ten

Seven countries of Central America

Costa Rica
Belize
Guatemala
Honduras
Nicaragua
Panama
El Salvador

Eleven

Six Points for Ethical Behavior from author and philosopher Harry Emerson Fosdick

Is it reasonable?
Is it responsible?
Is it fair?
Will I think well of myself?
How would my hero do it?
Is it honest?

Twelve

International Phonetic Alphabet (Part One)

alpha
bravo
Charlie
delta
echo
foxtrot
golf
hotel

Thirteen

International Phonetic Alphabet (Part Two)

India
Juliet
kilo
Lima
Mike
November
Oscar
papa
Quebec

Fourteen

International Phonetic Alphabet (Part Three)

Romeo
sierra
tango
uniform
Victor
whisky
X-ray
yankee
Zulu

Fifteen

Rogers and Hammerstein Musicals

Oklahoma
Carousel
State Fair
Allegro
South Pacific
The King and I
Me and Juliet
Pipe Dream
Cinderella
Flower Drum Song
The Sound of Music

Sixteen

Random Words

savior
messenger
egg
lodge
pride
night
fall
hope
bishop
picture

Seventeen

Random Words

trousers
baton
lens
second
shoelace
noun
lobster
feast
belt
stool

Eighteen

Random Words

food
suicide
capsicum
coat
election
frown
honey
zebra
pail
athletics

Nineteen

Random Words

perfume
scorpion
crumbs
misnomer
wardrobe
souvenir
benefit
tartan
baby
tar

Twenty

Random Words

match
thermostat
gate
funeral
flywheel
price
sale
seed
fashion
cult

Twenty-One

Random Words

tape
statue
committee
carriage
taxi
flag
scream
gate
horse
fairy tale

Twenty-Two

Random Words

artist
prophet
carpenter
tattoo
trousers
sausage
juice
thunder
choir
pants

Twenty-Three

Random Words

harp
gallery
resting
tray
tablet
gallows
decoy
dice
trumpet
shoehorn

Twenty-Four

Random Words

asylum
sheet
value
holly
star
aid
wardrobe
intriguing
bet
union

Twenty-Five

Random Words

evening
consonant
joke
stage
icon
hope
spar
cup
cereal
miser

Twenty-Six

Random Words

war
whistle
boots
coronation
concierge
toast
sunrise
gnome
sand
chimpanzee

Twenty-Seven

Random Words

mattress
cherry
circus
chewing gum
riddle
fur
spar
cup
meadow
tourist

Twenty-Eight

Random Words

headline
advertising
powder
music
conference
juice
junk
egg
glasses
commander

Twenty-Nine

Random Words

comet
tomb
vowel
ring
cook
onion
fight
plaster
arrow
exile

Thirty

Random Words

paw
merit
clippers
suicide
trumpet
pencil
girders
switch
cult
ball

Printed in Great Britain
by Amazon

34038520R00047